CONTENTS

Page 4   The Solar System

Page 6   What Are the Planets?

Page 8   Earth

Page 10   Mercury and Venus

Page 12   Mars

Page 14   Jupiter

Page 16   Saturn

Page 18   Uranus and Neptune

Page 20   Dwarf Planets

Page 22   Perfect Planets!

Page 24   Glossary and Index

THE SECRET BOOK COMPANY

©2018
The Secret Book
Company
King's Lynn
Norfolk PE30 4LS

ISBN: 978-1-912171-74-3

Written by:
Gemma McMullen
Edited by:
Harriet Brundle
Designed by:
Drue Rintoul
Ian McMullen

A catalogue record for this book
is available from the British Library.

Words in **bold** can be found in the glossary on page 24.

MERCURY AND VENUS

Mercury is the closest planet to the Sun. It has a rocky surface with large craters. Mercury is very hot on the side closest to the Sun.

Venus is the hottest planet. It is even hotter than Mercury because it is covered in clouds that keep heat in. It is the closest planet to Earth.

MARS

Mars is the fourth closest planet to the Sun. It is made from rock and is covered in red dust. For this reason, it is sometimes called the Red Planet.

Mars is a cold planet. Scientists have been able to send special vehicles called rovers to Mars to take pictures.

ROVER

JUPITER

Jupiter is the largest planet in the Solar System. It is a lot bigger than the other planets. Jupiter is mostly made of gas.

Jupiter has over 50 moons orbiting it. Jupiter's largest moon is called Ganymede. Ganymede is bigger than the planet Mercury!

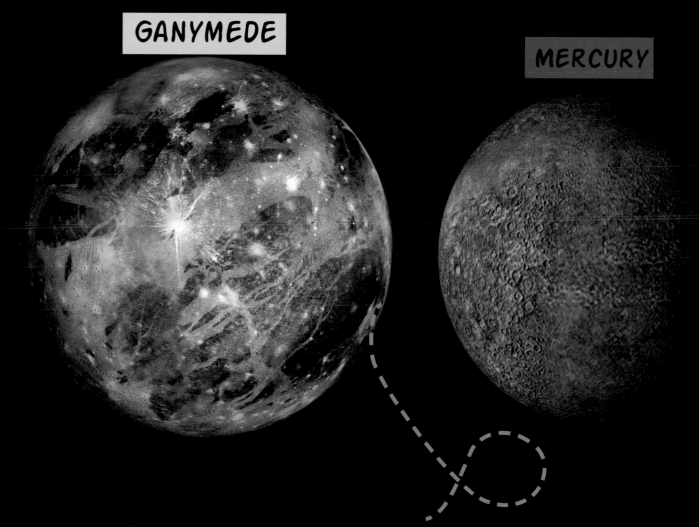

GANYMEDE

MERCURY

Space crafts have successfully visited Jupiter and some of its moons.

SATURN

Saturn is a giant gas planet. It has millions of pieces of rock and ice orbiting it, which makes it look as though Saturn has rings around it.

Saturn has over 50 moons, including the second largest in the whole Solar System. Space crafts have been sent to orbit Saturn and send pictures to scientists.

URANUS AND NEPTUNE

Uranus is a large gas planet. It is a cold planet. Uranus spins in a different direction to the other planets, which makes it seem as though it has fallen onto its side.

Neptune is the farthest planet from the Sun. Like Uranus, it is a cold gas planet. Only one space craft has visited Neptune.

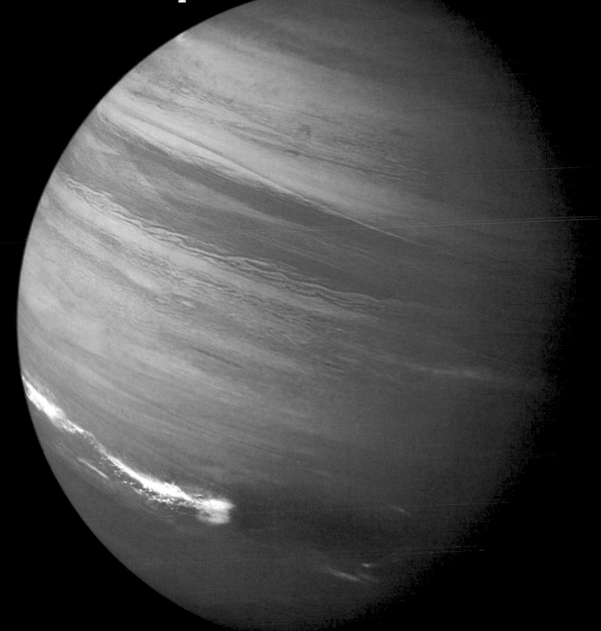

DWARF PLANETS

Dwarf planets are round and orbit the Sun, but they are much smaller than the eight planets. Dwarf planets are even smaller than Earth's moon.

Pluto is a dwarf planet. It used to be one of the main planets, but in 2006 scientists decided it was a dwarf planet.

EARTH

PLUTO

Many dwarf planets have moons of their own.

PERFECT PLANETS!

Venus is the brightest planet in our sky and can sometimes be seen without even using a **telescope**.

Jupiter is so big that you could fit all the other planets inside it.

Every so often, Mercury can be seen crossing the Sun.

MERCURY

Neptune has the most stormy weather out of all of the planets.

23

GLOSSARY

asteroids	large rocks that orbit the Sun
craters	large holes shaped like bowls
dwarf planets	very small planets
equator	an imaginary line on planet Earth which shows the hottest part
orbit	move around
telescope	a tool used to make viewing distant objects easier

INDEX

dwarf planets 5, 20-21
Earth 4, 6, 8-9, 11, 20
Jupiter 6, 14-15, 22
Mars 6, 12-13
Mercury 6-7, 10-11, 15, 23
moons 5, 15, 17, 20-21
Neptune 6, 18-19, 23

Pluto 21
Saturn 6, 16-17
Solar System 4-5, 14, 17
Sun 4-5, 6-7, 10, 12, 19, 20, 23
Uranus 6, 18-19
Venus 6- 7, 10-11, 22

PHOTO CREDITS

Photocredits: Abbreviations: l-left, r-right, b-bottom, t-top, c-centre, m-middle. All images are courtesy of Shutterstock.com.
Front Cover — Aphelleon. 1, 10, 24inset – Vadim Sadovski. 2 – cigdem. 3 – nienora. 4-5 – fluidworkshop. 5br – Denis_A. 6-7 – Johan Swanepoel. 8inset – Tyler Olson. 9 – Michelangelus. 12 – Stephen Girimont 13 – Marc Ward. 14 – Ksanawo. 15l – Tristan3D. 15r – CVADRAT. 16 – Denis_A. 17inset – MarcelClemens. 17 – AS Food studio. 18 – 3DMaestro 19 – Tristan3D. 21inset – Claudio Divizia. 22 – Javier Rosano 23inset – Kenneth Sponsler. 23 – Marc Ward. All facts, statistics, web addresses and URLs in this book were verified as valid and accurate at time of writing. No responsibility for any changes to external websites or references can be accepted by either the author or publisher.